NATIVE NAMES

of

NEW ENGLAND

TOWNS and VILLAGES

TRANSLATING 211 NAMES
DERIVED FROM NATIVE AMERICAN WORDS

Third Edition

Second Printing

C. Lawrence Bond, A.B., S. B.

Illustrations by Pat Lucas
Edited by Alan B. Bond

2003
Rochester, Vermont

ii

NATIVE NAMES OF NEW ENGLAND TOWNS AND VILLAGES,
Translating 211 Names Derived From Native American Words by C.
Lawrence Bond

For information address Alan B. Bond, Publisher and Editor

First Edition Copyright 1991 by C. Lawrence Bond
Second Edition Copyright 1993 Alan B.Bond
Third Edition Copyright 2000 Alan B. Bond
Third Edition, Second Printing 2003

ISBN: 0-9638180-2-3
LIBRARY OF CONGRESS LOCATOR NUMBER
00 130429

Address: Native Names
P.O. Box 67
Rochester, Vermont 05767

Layout and Editing by Alan B. Bond

INTRODUCTION

Some forty years ago I was employed, as a civil engineer, checking on the property of a public utility that took me all over southern Maine. The number of towns with Native American names interested me, and so I started a card index with such information as I could pick up relative to the meaning. Unfortunately, I did not always keep a reference as to the source, so there are some gaps in my glossary at the end of this booklet.

There have been innumerable books written on the subject, most of which are out of print. I have been fortunate in my ability to pick up some of the most important and helpful books in second hand bookstores. With these I was able to get the linguistic roots, and with some knowledge of the topography, make a reasonable translation.

There were as many dialects within the Algonkian language of New England as there were tribes. Before the arrival of Europeans Indians did not write, and, for the most part, the colonists were not experts at writing down what they thought the names sounded like. Consequently, there were many variations in spelling the Indian place names.

In 1989 I finished writing *A History of the Houses and Buildings of Topsfield* (Massachusetts) for the local Historical Society, and determined to put my Indian notes into some useful form. Using an automobile tourist map, I jotted down all the town names in the index that appeared to be of Indian origin. Names of brooks, ponds and mountains do not show in the index. There are so many that I doubt I should ever get through them. I should point out that the names of many towns have been adopted from Indian named brooks, ponds or bays.

I make no claim to being a philologist, and am open-minded as to my findings based on the work of others, but I am not bashful about criticizing meanings given without reason.

John Eliot made the first translation of the Bible into an Indian tongue in 1663. J. H. Trumbull took Eliot's Natick Bible as the source of his Natick Dictionary which includes English translation to Natick.

F. H. Eckstorm goes to great lengths to explore roots. She knew four Indian families in Old Town. If each one gave a different meaning she knew it was only saving face. If two agreed she thought it had value, but if three agreed she felt confident in the meaning.

Joseph Laurent was chief of an Abenaki tribe. I met and corresponded with his son, who autographed and gave me one of his father's dictionaries.

Reider T. Sherwin makes a very good claim for some names having a Norse basis. Samuel Eliot Morison, the Harvard historian, proved that Lief Erikson never got to New England. Morison commented, however, that a Norse bishop set out to take Christianity to Vinland, and was never heard from again. He could have lost his way, been shipwrecked somewhere along the coast and his crew eventually married with Indians. Four hundred years can blot out a lot of memories! It is only my speculation. My historical experience is limited to the Essex County Courthouse and the Topsfield Town Hall, but the apparent Norse root to Indian words certainly stimulates the imagination!

The Indians were not unlikely to elide or even eliminate some syllables in forming a descriptive name. It is quite probable that the colonials made over syllables to make a name more easily pronounced. It may, therefore, appear that some writers have had to make some wild guesses at the original word in order to fit the topography. If I have used a dialectical term in an area where it is not usual, I can only say that I have no vocabulary for the locus that helps. I am open to your criticism.

C. Lawrence Bond
Topsfield, Massachusetts
1991

INTRODUCTION TO THE THIRD EDITION

In the 95th year of his life C. Lawrence Bond made fifty additional entries to the book. He wrote, "Many of the additions represent significant rivers, mountains, lakes and bays or geographical features of particular interest. It is my hope that those who use this little reference book will enjoy learning about this aspect of the history of New England and will more deeply appreciate the Native American culture which gave the area so many names."

The on-going interest in this effort has encouraged me to invite Pat Lucas to enhance its appearance with interpretive drawings, add a name or two and make some corrections.

Alan B. Bond, Editor
Reading, Massachusetts
January 2000

PREFACE

This little book is organized in such a way as to provide easy reference to towns in New England with names of Native American origin. They are listed by state, north to south and in the following order:

Name

       Etymology (The ≈ indicates an equivalent or alternate spelling) Dialect
       Meaning
       Explanation (where appropriate)
       Geographical Location
       Alternative meaning and alternative source
       Notes

Where an earlier definition has been found that does not conform to the etymology here given, the initials of the author(s) are given.

The following is an identification of the initials of the authors:

AGW	Alvin G. Weeks
ENH	Eben N. Horsford
FHE	Fannie Hardy Eckstorm
JCH	John C. Huden
JHT 1, 2, 3	J. Hammond Trumbull
JL	Joseph Laurent
LLH	Lucius L. Hubbard
MFS	M. F. Sweetser
RAD-L	R.A. Douglass-Lithgow
RTS 1, 2	Reider T. Sherwin
SR	(Father) Sabastian Rasles
WFG	Warner F. Gookin

A Bibliography of their books appears at the rear of this booklet.

No attempt has been made to provide a complete dictionary of Indian words or names, or of brooks, rivers and ponds, but it is important to recognize that many names describe the topography and waterways as seen from a canoe going upstream. A "Sachem" is a tribal chief.

The Glossary of root syllables is in two parts, representing words from northern and southern New England. In committing Indian names to English it was not easy to distinguish 'b' and 'p', 'd' and 't', 'g' and 'k', 'l' and 'r', and the vowels are equally interchangeable.

Any effort to reduce native language to written form is bound to fail to some degree. Native language, like some Asian languages depends on intonation, inflection and physical gesture. It is the author's hope that these efforts have done no violence to the original tongues or the names of places which follow.

ABOUT THE COVER MAP

A reproduction of the first map cut in America graces our cover. It was originally published in William Hubbard's *Narrative of the Troubles with the Indians in New England* (Boston, 1677). Samuel Abbott Green has remarked: "Unlike the common way of showing the cardinal points, the top of the map represents the West, and the bottom represents the East. There are two heavy lines drawn up and down... which are intended to mark the boundaries of the Massachusetts Colony. The charter, it will be remembered, gave the Company all the land lying between a parallel three miles south of any part of the Charles River, and a similar parallel three miles north of the Merrimack River; and these lines were supposed to bound this territory." Somehow, Hubbard managed to include a sizable chunk of Plymouth Colony in Bay territory, an error some anonymous editor tried to correct by running a smaller line from Medfield to Scituate. See Green, T*en Fac-simile Reproductions Relating to Old Boston and Neighborhood* (Boston, 1901). We are grateful to the Congregational Library, 14 Beacon St., Boston, for its help in locating a copy of the print.

A FURTHER NOTE FROM THE EDITOR

Shortly before the second printing of the Third Edition we learned of the Language Reclamation Project being undertaken by the Wampanoag Nation and under the guidance of Jessie Little Doe. The work of the project makes it evident that the historic translations by English speaking people and found in this volume fall short of accuracy or do not do justice to the original tongues. In the spirit of the efforts of my father, we will be supportive of the project. We hope to eventually publish more accurate translations and meanings when the L.R.P. work becomes available. In the meantime it is our hope that this effort will continue to deepen an appreciation for the role Native people have played in providing all of us with meaningful names of places in our region.

Alan B. Bond, Editor

AGAMENTICUS

Agamen - other side island **wki tuk** - river **s** - diminutive.
(Abenaki)

Small river other side of island

The Pisquataqua is the chief river. To an Indian coming in from the open sea, what is now called the York River would be the small river on the other side of the island.

FHE goes to great lengths to disqualify many other translations, after viewing the area from a canoe. The name has been applied to a pond and a mountain some miles further into Maine. An example of the use of an Indian name with no significance to present use.

ALLAGASH

(w)alagaskoo - bark; **k** is a location suffix.
(Abenaki)

Bark place

Village, river and falls southwest of Fort Kent at the principal fork of the St. John River.
"Bark cabin lake" RAD-L
RAD-L suggests the name was probably shortened from "alligaskigamo." Birch bark was used in canoes as well as cabins.

ANDROSCOGGIN

(N)ahmays - fish, **congin** - curing
(Abenaki)

Fish curing

River rising in N.H., flows into Merrymeeting Bay. The name undoubtedly referred to the rocks in Brunswick.
The author thinks there may have been a purposeful slur in the pronunciation. Andros was a very unpopular Colonial Governor in the early eighteenth century.

ANNABESACOOK

Anna - (not found, probably an adjective such as clear or smooth) **be**- contraction of nip(pe) - river, **saco** ≈ - outlet **ook** - locative, indicative of pool.
(Abenaki)

Smooth water at outlet

A lake in Monmouth.
If the smooth water was caused by a weir, it was probably a quarter of a mile downstream based on U.S.G.S. contours. The lake is now called Wilson and a railroad station of the name has long since disappeared.
Alternative: Where small fish are caught.

AROOSTOOK

(W)alas - shallow (note: 'l' and 'r' are interchangeable.) **s** - (connective) **took** ≈ **tegw** - river.
(Micmac)

Shallow river

County in northern Maine and a long river.

1. Shining River. JCH
2. Beautiful river. RAD-L
Laurent's Dictionary 206
The name probably originally described the junction between the river and the St. John's River in New Brunswick. Stephen Laurent gives us the translation "Shallow River"" but it seems misapplied for the largest county!

BUNGAMUG
(Original spelling was BUNGOMUNGOMUG)

Bungomun ≈ **gomug** - boundary
(Abenaki)

Boundary

A river in Yarmouth ; a boundary between
Brunswick and Freeport.
JHT suggests that the name signifies that it is non-
residential, that is a town bound.

CAPE NEDDICK   (See NEDDICK)

CAPE NEWAGEN   (See NEWAGEN)

CARABASSET

Kah - sharp, splintery, **apskw** - rocks, **set** - (locus)
Sharp rock place

Sturgeon place. JHC
According to Mrs. Eckstorm in "John Neptune"
the word was the name of an Indian captain, but
anyone who has seen the rocks at the mouth of
the river would know that the Indians must have
had a name of it."

CARATUNK

Cara ≈ kara - scraped; **tunk** ≈ tuun - enclosure, -
k location. (Abenaki or possibly Norse)

Scraped field

Where caribou scrape snow to find grass.
Village on the Kennebec River above Bingham.

CARIBOU

The shoveler
(Abenaki)

Caribou pawed the ground for food.
To the northwest of Fort Fairfield.
The word was not used by Indians for a place.

CASCO

Helmet (Spanish)

Bay off Portland.
The name is not Indian. It was given by Estaban Gomez in 1525. In Spanish "casco" means helmet. A helmet used to have a visor with slits.
The estuaries were the slits, the long points were the visor.

CATHANCE

Cath ≈ keht - principal; **ance** ≈ anis - branch
(Abenaki)

Principal branch

A branch off Merrymeeting Bay, considered part of the Kennebec River.
River and village in Topsham.

CHEBEAGUE

Chebe ≈ sebe - divided or almost through; **-ague** - beneath (Abenaki)

Literally "**divided**" or "**almost through beneath**"

At high tide it becomes two islands.
Island in Casco Bay.
FHE page 255 It is difficult to translate literally because it refers to a condition at low tide when there was no passageway between.

COBBOSSEECONTEE

Kabasse - sturgeon;   **kantti** - plenty (A transliteration) (Abenaki)

Sturgeon plenty

Stream and lake at Gardiner.
Not truly a place name without a suffix to denote water.

CUPISSIC

Kep - stopped up, **piske** - branch (Abenaki)

Impassable branch (of a river)

Small stream in Deering (Portland).

CUSHNOC (ACCUSHENOC)

Ak - above, **ushen** ≈ **sjoe** - ocean or tide, **oc** - locative ending
(Norse or Abenaki)

Place above the tide.

No longer found on maps it was an old name for Augusta.
This translation has been recognized for a long time, but no one knew the etymology of the word. CLB found it in Accushnet, Massachusetts as a Norse based word and recognized the similarity to the translation. Salt water does not reach Augusta, but the tidal rise in Merrymeeting Bay causes the Kennebec to back up as far as the falls in East Augusta.

DAMARISCOTTA

(Not an Indian word.) (English?)
Humphrey Damarell and a John Cotta lived in the area. Possibly their names were combined.

Cove, lake and village east of Bath.
Dr. Ganong, Royal Society of Ottawa says "It seems to me the name is not Indian at all."
(Transactions Vol IX))
Modern Indians called the area
"(Ma)demesconte."
FHE points out there is no "n" in Damariscotta nor location suffix.

KATADIN

Kehte - great, outstanding **adn** - mountain
(Abenaki)

Great mountain

Twelve or fifteen miles north of Lake
Millinocket.

KENDUSKEAG

Kad ≈ kat - eel; **esq** ≈ esog - weir; **keag** ≈ quit -
place or reef. (Maliseet)

Eel weir place

River near Bangor, tributary to the Penobscot.

FHE says on page 15 that an earlier spelling was
"Kadequit."

KENNEBAGO

Kenne - long; **bago** ≈ bagw, ≈ begat - still water. (Abenaki)

Long pond

The long pond from which village and mountain were named, but not by the Indians.
Lake, mountain and village near Rangely.

KENNEBEC

Kenne - long; **bec** (k) still water or reach. (Abenaki)

Long reach

From above Merrymeeting Bay to Augusta.
The river from Moosehead Lake to Popham Beach.

KENNEBUNK

Kenne - long; **bunk** ≈ benek - cut bank, = (Abenaki)

Long cut bank

Cut bank as seen from the sea.
Village and River southwest of Biddeford.
Dr. Ganong indicates it is Micmac.

KINEO

(see note below)
(possibly Norse)

Moose rock

Northeast shore of Moosehead Lake, opposite the western outlet.
The name was applied to a village nearby.

1. ""Sharp rock"" JCH p. 20
According to legend, was the body of moose killed by Gluskehbeh.

KOKADJO

Koh - kettle; **adjo** ≈ Adchu ≈ adne - mountain.
(Abenaki, but "koh" is not of this dialect.)

Kettle mountain

Village and Mountain northeast of Moosehead Lake.
JCH says a legend holds that Glooscap killed a moose which became Mt. Kineo, then pursued the calf. To lighten his load he threw down his kettle which became the mountain.

MACHIAS

Matchi - bad; **ia** ≈ ya - run of water; **s** indicates "small" (Abenaki)

A little run of bad water

Town and river near the Bay of Fundy.
"Bad little falls" JCH

MACWAHOC

(T)**makwa** - beaver; **hoc** - place.
(Abenaki)

Beaver place

A stream outletting in the Molunkus, and the
name of a village at the junction of Routes 2 and
170.
"Wet ground" JCH

MAD A KAMIGO SEK

Mad ≈ **mag** - big, **kamigo** - high ridge
(Micmac)

Big high ridge

North of Camden.
This name does not appear on current maps but
the syllables appear in the Glossary.

MADAWASKA

Mada - poor, worn out; **ask** - grass; (askash -
green JHT) (Micmac)

Worn out grass(land)

Village and river (separate).
Opposite Edmonton, New Brunswick.
"Where one river runs into another" JCH

MADOMCOOK
MEDUMCOOK

Med ≈ met - at the end of , umc - sand bar,
ook - pool, harbor or bay. (FHE 21)
(Abenaki)

Bay at the end of the sand bar

Probably indicative of a fishing place.
It is located in Friendship
Because of earlier translations Mrs. Eckstorm
prefers the second spelling and gives the fore-
going definition.
CLB prefers "**big mountain stream.**"

MAGUNTICOOK

Mag - big, un ≈ adn - mountain, cook - pool
or harbor
(Maliseet)

Big mountain harbor

Camden

MAGWINTEGWAK

Megwin - a swelling, tegwak - waves
(Mailiseet)

Choppy seas

Off Lincolnville.
Fr. O'Brian.

MALAGA ISLAND

Maladagw - cedar
(St. Francis dialect)

Cedar (Island)

A small island near the western shore of
Phippsburg
Fr. Rasles

MANANSIS ISLAND

Manan - Island, sis - small
(Micmac or Maliseet)

Small Island

Opposite Monhegan.

MANSET

Man - island; **s** - small; **et** - at (Abenaki)

At small island

Near Mt. Desert.
"At the island" JCH
In Massachusetts "man" indicates a lookout.

MARANACOOK

Mar - is not found in any dialect: It may be an
Indian's name combined with a suffix to denote
where he lived. **cook ≈ ook** - pool or bay.

Bay

A lake which lies between Winthrop and
Readville, and a village which lies midway
along the lake.
If "Marana" is a transposition of "Manan" -
island, then the meaning would be "bay island."
Some canoeist, familiar with the lake, may be able
to identify a feature not disclosed in its
etymology.

MASARDIS

Masar ≈ maza - white, **-dis** (not found)
(Abenaki)

White clay

Town on Route 11, west of Presque Isle. JL

MATINICUS

Matin ≈ metin - cut off, separate; **nic** ≈ nighe -
island (Abenaki)

Far off island

An island twenty miles off Isle au Haut.
"Far out island" JCH
FHE ascribes the final 's' as the Penobscot soft-
ened location ending 'k'.
Champlaine called Isle au Haut, "isles jette."

MATTAWAMKEAG

Matta - at the mouth; **w** (- a connective);
amkeag - sand bar (Abenaki)

At the sand bar at the junction
 (of the Penobscot River)

Route 2 north east of Lincoln.
"Fishing place beyond gravel bar", or "rapids at
 mouth"JCH
A lake at the source forty miles away also bears
 the name which indicates 'matta' may prop-
 erly translate "at end of."

MEDDYBEMPS

Meddy ≈ medames - alewives; **bem** ≈ pem -
extended (Abenaki)

Extensive area for alewives

Lake and village on route 191 northeast of
Eastport.
"Plenty of alewives"   JCH
An earlier form was "Meddybemscook," the
ending indicating flowing water, probably
rapids.

MEDOMAK

Medom ≈ medames - alewives; **ac** (- locative
ending) (Abenaki)

Place for (fishing) **alewives**

River and village in Waldoboro
"Place of many alewives"JCH
Of note is the fact that the accent is on the sec-
ond syllable.

MERRICONEAG

Merru - swift or quick, **coneag** -contraction of **ounegan** - portage
(Abenaki)

Place for quick portage

Once applied to Harpswell Neck, but later transferred to the Sound.
Francis Stanislaus suggest if the rr's are sounded as ll's, as the Malecites do, the word means a lazy carry. That is one where the canoes are not unloaded, but dragged across.

MILLINOCKET

Mille ≈ molle - deep; **nock** ≈ tatnock - marshy place **et** (- locative ending) (Abenaki)

At the deep marsh grass

Town, lake and hill, northerly end Route 11.
1. "This place admirable," or "many coves," or "broken by out-jutting rocks and islands." JCH
2. "Having no shape," or "having many coves," or "place full of islands." RAD-L
It is obvious that an Indian name has been applied to other than the original place.

MOLUNKUS

Molanke - ravine   (Abenaki)

Ravine

Name of a stream, a lake and a village on Route 2, west of Macwahoc.

MONHEGAN

Monhe ≈ mone - island, **gan** ≈ egon - out to sea (Maliseet)

Island out to sea
Twenty miles off Pemaquid.
"Grand Island" RADL
See Dr. Ganong .

MONTSWEAG

Mon ≈ **mud** - dug (steep sided), **sweag** ≈ **sege** - narrows.
(Abenaki)

Narrow channel

Bay and brook in the Sheepscot river, and name of a village on Route 1, southwest of Wiscasset.
1. Dug out channel   JHC

MOOSELOOKMEGUNTIC

Moosi - smooth, **meguntic** ≈ **megwin** - a swelling, **tegwak** - waves

Smooth when choppy seas

One of the Rangeley lakes.
CLB finds no etymology for the 'look" but the geography of the region would explain why the place might have smooth water during choppy waves in the main lake. However, if the "l" is a later insertion then "ook" which denotes water would make sense.

MUSCONGUS

(Nah)mas - fish, **congu** -curing, **s** - locative ending

Fish curing place

The name of an island and applied to a sound below Waldoboro.

NASKEAG

Nas ≈ **nahmas** - fish, **keag** - point
(St. Francis dialect)

Fish point

Alternative: **N'** - at, **ask** - point ; **keag** -point.
Hence: at the point of the point, i.e. the end.
FHE states that no Penobscot Indian could explain
"ask." Perhaps it is a transcript from the French
maps.

NEDDICK

Nadwk - nubble (Micmac)

A standing stone pillar

The name applies to nubble off shore.
Part of York.
Dr. Ganong.

NEQUASSETT

Nequa - only, **s** - (probably all that is left of
sebem - pond) **et** - at
(Abenaki)

At the only pond (in the area)

However, it might be """The only spring.""""
The pond is so little above the bank of the
Kennebec it may be salty at flood tides.

NEWAGEN, Cape

Anglicized form for CHAUGHNAWAGA
Ca ≈ ke - where; **ohnawa** - swift current;
ga (- location ending place)

Place where there is a swift current

There is a narrow strait between Southport and
the Cape.
An island part of Southport.
"Closed route"RADL and FHE
FHE goes to great length to explain what she
thinks was meant by a closed route.
This author asks, why name a land route for an
unspecified closed one?
JL says the root word is Iroquois.

OGUNQUIT

Pog ≈ paug - pond; **umkik** ≈ amkeag ≈ unquit -
sand bar (Abenaki)

A sand bar lagoon at river mouth.

River, falls and village in Wells.
"Lagoons within dunes or place of waves."
JCH
The author's definition agrees with FHE, but not
exactly her etymology.
Dr. Ganong suggests that it is Micmac,
Pogumkik: "a lagoon formed by sand dunes."

OLAMON

≈ vermilion (Abenaki)
Coloring for war paint was obtained there.
Island at the junction of the Olamon River west
of the Penobscot and 14 miles above Milford.

"Paint place" RAD-L

OQUOSSOCO

Oquo ≈ **acco** - other side, **s-** diminutive, **soc** ≈
sook (indicating) water
(Abenaki)

Place at other side of little stream

A stream connecting Rangeley and
Mooselookmeguntic lakes.

ORONO

(A person's name.)
Between Bangor and Old Town
Jos. Orono (d. 1801) at an estimated age of over
113 years. Supposedly related to Castine, he had
blue eyes and red hair.

PASSADUMKEAG

Passad (is an unusual root in place names) ≈ of
pansitwiwi - above **umkeag** - sandbar (Maliseet)

Locus above the sandbar, that is, **upstream**

Village and river east of Penobscot River, north
of Old Town.
1. "Beyond the sand beach" RAD-L
2. "Falls over gravel bed" LLH
3. "Rapids over gravel bed" JCH;
The present town is not on the site of the Indian
village. I see nothing that indicates 'falls' as
suggested by the alternatives.

PASSAMAQUODDY

Peska tum - pollock jumping, **quaddy** ≈ **contee** - plenty

Plenty pollock jumping

The great bay at Eastport.
FHE says that the pollock, while pursuing smaller fish, leap clear out of the water, reversing at once, so that the bays seems full of fishes standing on their heads."

PEJEPSCOT

Pe ≈ pem - extensive; **jep** ≈ idge - rapids; **scot** ≈ apske - rock (Abenaki)

Long rocky rapids

Village between Topsham and Lisbon on the Androscoggin River.
In the 1700s an Indian, Pierpole, indicated the name applied to the whole twenty miles from Brunswick to Lewiston, but present day dams have obscured the rapids.

PEMAQUID

Pema - extended or far out; **quid** - ≈ equid - it is situated (Abenaki - Micmac dialect)

It is far out (toward the sea)

Point and Village south of Damariscotta.
FHE 103 suggests the etymology for the word.
Dr. Ganong believed it was Micmac.

PENOBSCOT

Pen - fall from height; **obsc** ≈ apsk - rock; **ot** locative ending. (Penobscot - Maliseet dialect)

At the rocky slope

River, bay and village, the latter being west of Blue Hill.
FHE indicates the fall of height is known to have applied over a distance, i.e. a slope. Now the name applies to the river all the way to Millenocket and the Bay all the way to the open sea.

QUODDY

See Passamaquoddy

RIPOGENUS

So far as known it was an invented name when Wyman Dam was built.

SABATTUS

Named for an Indian who accompanied Arnold to Quebec.
The name is the Abenaki version of **St. Jean Baptiste.**
Village, Pond and River north of Lewiston.

SACO

Not an Indian name

It was called Bahia de Saco (**Bay of the Sack**) by Estaban Gomez in 1525.
Biddeford Pool on the south side of the bay is a distinctive feature, and is truly a sack.
     Town and bay.
FHE goes to great length trying to show some Indian words from which it was derived. See FHE 170-2

SAGADAHOC

Sada ≈ **sauk** - outlet, **da** -(etymology not given) **hoc** - swift current

Place where strong current flows out

County.
FHE
The name is applicable to the mouth of the Kennebec River.

SAPONAC

Sa ≈ chi - big; **pon** - spread (out); **ac** ≈ ook -water place. (Abenaki)

Spread out water place.

The original word, Chibanook, was applied to the first widening of a stream as one moved up stream.
Lake and Village 10 or 12 miles up the Passadumkeag River, northeast of Old Town.

"The great outlet," or "Big opening" JCH
The translation of the first syllable is from FHE 50.
The present village is not on the original site.

SEBAGO

(me)si - great; **begat** - still water (Abenaki)

Great Lake

Source of the Presumpscot River.
Lake and Village part of Standish.
"Big still water"JCH
See also FHE page 161 -2.

SEBASCODEGAN

Sebes - almost through, **co** ≈ **(aps)co** - rock, **d** - place, **egan** - passage

Rocky passage almost through

Short carry for a canoe.
Former name of Great Island

SEBASTOCOOK

Sebes - almost through, **ticook** ≈ **tegw** - river

Almost through passage river

Tributary to the Kennebec River at Winslow.
The tributary served as the shortest route to the Penobscot, used by Arnold on his way to Quebec.

SEBEC

Se ≈ **(m)si** - large; **bec** ≈ **begek** - pond (Abenaki)

Large pond

North of Dover-Foxcroft.
"Much water" JCH

SEBOEIS

Sebo(e) - brook; (s)**is** - little (Abenaki)

Little brook

Stream, lake and village north of Howland
"Small lake or waterway" JCH
As in many Maine place names, the Indian word
has been used for the name of a village which
may never have been there in Indian times.
See also JL page 40.

SHEEPSCOT

(Pah)**she** -divided; **apske** - rock; **ot** - locative
ending. (Abenaki)

At the split rock

River, pond and village west of Newcastle.
1. "Divided by many rocks" FHE;
2. "Many rocky channels" JCH;
3. "bird flocking river"   RAD-L
The author asks, "Is there a split rock here?" He
hesitates to refute FHE, but there is nothing in
'scot' that indicates a plurality of rocks. She refers to 'tortuous byways' of the river. (See FHE
page 159)
For the first syllable see FHE page 115.

SKOWHEGAN

Skow ≈ Erasko - watching; **hegan** ≈ egon -
ridge (Abenaki)

Place for watching for fish

Town and falls on upper Kennebec River.
"Fish spearing place" JCH
See also Dr. Ganong.

TOGUS (WILLAMA)TOGUS

A corruption of Waliniticus   **Walini** - curve or
cove, **ticus** ≈ **tegw** - river

River cove

Part of Pittston (see note).
The name was applied to part of Pittston in early
Massachusetts archives, but FHE shows the
name derives from a stream and cove above
Castine.

WALLAGRASS

Walagaskw - bark   (Abenakis)

Place to find birch bark. (SL page 32)

Village 10 miles south of Canadian border.
The lake is no where near it.
If Micmac, then "good river";
If Abenakis, then "full of coves". JCH
Nothing indicates an Indian village.
See Allagash.

WHISKEAG

Whish - (probably reminiscent of a term for) grass grown creek, **keag** - at a point of land

Grass grown creek at point of land   FHE

Part of West Bath.
FHE points out this is difficult to pin-point as to origin, but indicates that the idea is a creek that runs dry at low tide, so that it becomes grass grown.

WILLIMANTIC

Willi ≈ wili - good; **man** - look out or island; **tic** ≈ tigw -stream or river. (Abenakis)

A good watch place on the stream

Village west of Lake Sebec.
"Cedar swamp" JCH
See JL page 65; FHE page 97; JL page 16.

WINNEGANCE

Winne - smooth or clear, **gan** - passageway, **ce** - locative suffix

A clear passage or portage

West Bath, a branch off the Kennebec and applied to the bay east of Harpswell.

WISCASSET

Wisca ≈ wetchi - whence comes out; **set** - near
the place (Abenakis)

"Comes out from but you don't see where"
FHE 119

The Sheepscot River is fresh water above and
tidal below, but the junction is not seen from
downstream. Town at the junction of Routes 1
and 27
"Hidden outlet"   JCH
The 1662 spelling, Wichcasset, changed in 1786
to the present form.
"Wisc" is the softened equivalent of "wetch", an
outlet differing from "sauk" in that it is obscured.
The present village center is downstream from
the junction described.
The first syllable is interpreted by Rev. M.
O'Brian.

WYTOPITLOCK

Wytopi ≈ Wdopi - alder tree; **tl** (not explained);
ock - place

Alder tree place

Village 15 miles north of Springfield.
FHE on page 57 says, "There are twenty-eight
spellings of the name. There is a stream tributary
to the Mattawamkeag now named Wytopitlock, but
-ock is not a water suffix.

There is no explanation for the letters "tl"
found in conjunction with each other."

AGIOCOCHOOK

No etymology of the word. (see note)
(Abenakis)

White Mountains

Douglas-Lithgow lists it as this meaning.
"Place of concealed one " (referring to Mt.
Washington).
JCH provides the alternative from a shortened
word Agiochook.

AMOSKEAG

Amo ≈ Amau - fish, (combined with) **keag**
(becomes)a place to fish with hook and line, **s** -
in the middle would indicate a small point.
(Abenaki)

A place to fish with hook and line

As contrasted with fishing weirs.

ASHUELOT

(N)ashu - between   (Pennacook)

JHT 2 p. 6 does not give the rest of the etymology but indicates it refers to land in the crotch of
a river.
A pond and mountain in Washington, NH.
Villages in MA and CT as well.

ASQUAM

Asqua ≈ **askui** - green, **am** ≈ **um** makes a
noun. (Abenaki)

Green grass

Probably first applied to a river, then used for
the lake and mountain.
Salmon place. JCH

CHOCORUA

(Not an Indian place name.) (Pennacook)
Named for an Indian Sachem killed in peace
time.
Mountain and Lake west of Madison

CONTOOCOOK

Con ≈ (pa)cun - nut; **toocoo** ≈ tegw - river; **k**
(locative ending) - at or by. (Pennacook)

By the river where there are nut trees.

Village and river west of Concord.
1. "Nut tree river" JCH;
2. "Crow place or river." RAD-L
See also GMD in the Bibliography.

COOS

Cowas - pine tree (Abenaki)

Pine tree

The current name is a contraction of the Indian word .
Coos is the former name of Newbury and is the name of the County.

GONIC

(Squamma)gonic - salmon
Squa ≈ m'sqi - red; **ammago ≈ amaug** - fish;
ic - locative suffix. (Abenaki)

At the salmon fishing place.

Village near Rochester.
"Salmon spearing place." JCH

HOOKSETT

It is of doubtful Indian origin.
However, it is possibly (anna)**hook** - shell; **set** -
near. (Pennacook)

Originally an island in the river, south of Concord.
"At the place of beautiful trees." JCH
The earliest mention of Hookset is during the American Revolution.

MASSABESIC

Massa - great, **be ≈ pe** - water, **sic ≈ sauk** - outlet (Abenaki)

Great lake outlet

The ending indicates a place, not a lake.
Near Manchester.
1. Near the great brook JCH
2. At the great lake RAD-L

MONADNOCK

Mon ≈ **man** - island, **adn** ≈ **aten** - mountain, **ock** - locative suffix (Abenaki and Natick)

At the island (i.e. separate) **mountain**

Cheshire County.

NASHUA

Nashaue (a preposition) - halfway. (Pennacook)

Halfway

Nashua lies half way between the source and the mouth of the Merrimack River.
City and River in southern New Hampshire.

1. "Between streams." JCH
2. "Land between." RADL
See the comment in the Glossary of root meanings.

NUBANUSIT

Nuba ≈ **nuppoh** - a wing, **nusi** ≈ **(un)nussu** - shaped, **t** - locative ending (Abenaki)

At the wing shaped (pond)

The pond has an irregular shaped U with its bottom toward the north.
Lake in Hancock.

OSSIPPEE

Oss ≈ coos - pines; **sippe** - river. (Abenaki)

Pine river.
New Hampshire Town Names page 68.

Lake, village and mountain in mid-eastern N.H.

1. "Water on other side." JCH
2. "Island formed by enlargement of water." RAD-L
The name, first used in 1785 to designate a village was that of an Algonkian tribe.

PASSACONAWAY

(Pennacook)
Mountain named for a Pennacook Sachem.

PEMIGEWASSET

Pemi - extended, **ge** - denotes continuation,
wasset ≈ wasit - seething

Extended rapids

River opposite Winnepesaukee which it joins in
Franklin to form the Merrimack River

PENNACOOK

Penna - probably a transcription of **panna** with
suffix of **cook** which would indicate a river that
spread out as it approached a larger body of water (i.e. the Merrimack)

Name of a tribe
Former name of Concord.

SUNAPEE

(Has)**sun** - stone; **apee ≈** nipee - water.
  (Pennacook)

Stony pond

Village, lake and mountain in middle-west of
N.H.
"Rocks in water" RAD-L

SUNCOOK

(Has)**sun** - stone; **cook** - flowing water.
(Pennacook)

Stony channel

River and village southeast of Concord.
1. "At the rocky place." JCH
2. "At the rocks." RADL

WINNIPESAUKEE

Winne - good, smooth; **pe** ≈ (nip)pe - water; **saukee** - outlet. (Pennacook)

Good smooth water at outlet.

At its outlet the Winnepesaukee River is smooth where it joins the Pemigewasset (extended seething place) River. Indians liked to contrast names.
Central N.H.
The lake was obviously named for the river. There is no town by this name, but it is included because of its prominence.

NOTES

ASCUTNEY

Askui - green; **tne** ≈ edne - mountain;
ey - island. (Abenaki)

Green mountain monadnock

Village and mountain on side of the Connecticut
River.
1. "At the end of the river fork." JCH
2. "Fire mountain" (or) "Three brothers" RADL

MEMPHREMAGOG

Memphre ≈ **Mam aw** - long, **mago** ≈ **bago** -
lake, **g** ≈ **k** - locative suffix (Abenaki)

Long lake place

Lake that extends from Newport across the Canadian border.
SL claims these syllables are Abenaki, but they
differ from the Abenaki. terms used alone.

MISSISQUOI

Masipskoik (the word is not broken down)
(Abenaki)

Where there is flint

A river and bay connected to lake Champlain
and a National Wildlife Refuge south of
Route 2.
1. Big woman   RAD-L
2. Great grassy meadow   JCH

JL gives the meaning of the whole word. I can
find it in none of my books, but assume it is
French.

PASSUMPSIC

Pass - upstream, **umps** ≈ apsk - rock (Abenaki)

Upstream from rocky place

Village on Connecticut River near St. Johnsbury.
JL p. 217   JL writes "probably **pasomkasik,**"
a diminutive which means A 'river which has a
clear sandy bottom.'
The rocky place was probably where the
Comerford Dam is now located.

POMPANOOSUC (A contraction of Ompompanoosuc)

omp - man (in compound words); **panneussu** -
   wrong doer; **c** - locative   ending.
   (Abenakis)

Place of the bad man

River and village below Thetford.
"Quaky land." JCH
The author's interpretation suggests the name is
actually based on the Natick dialect. There is an
Abenaki word 'omanosek' which means 'fishing
place,' but I find no explanation for the 'omp-'
or the second letter 'p.'
For more on the etymology see JHT 3, pages
292, 100.

QUEECHEE (See Cochichiwick in Massachusetts)

Violent cascade

A gorge near the junction of routes 4 and 12, and
a nearby village.

WINOOSKI

Winos - onion; **ski** - land. (Abenakis)

Onion field

City north east of Burlington and a river.
"Wild onions" JCH

NOTES

ACOAXET

Acco - On other side; **ax** ≈ ak - land; **et** locative
ending. (Narragansett)

At land on other side.

As seen from Westport Point.
Southwest Massachusetts facing Rhode Island
Sound
1. At the fishing promontory.
2. A place of pines.
3. Small fields.
JCH suggests all three possibilities.

ACUSHNET

(Narragansett: Norse dialect? See note)

Head of tide.

The etymology of the name has never been de-
termined, but it appears to resemble Cushnoc in
Maine which Indians said meant "head of tide."
(See FHE page 145) This meaning fits both in
Massachusetts and Maine, but the suffix in both
implies land, not water .
North of Fairhaven.
Above tide.   RTS 1, page 8 and 322.
RTS suggests that it is Norse. Ak- above; sjoe -
sea (pronounced 'she'), hence, above tide.

AGAWAM

Agwe - beneath; **m** ≈ um (makes an adverb into
a noun.) (Pequakets)

Land beneath water. (Marshes)

The name is probably telescoped but all sources
agree on its meaning.
To the west side of the Connecticut River.
See JHT 3, page 225

AQUINNAH   The name recently applied to Gay Head on Martha's Vineyard. The etymology has not yet been provided by the Language Reclamation Project of the Wampanoag Nation.

ANNISQUAM

Wanashqua -

"At the top of a rock" Eliot's Bible

West side of Cape Ann
JHT's translation of Ezekiel 26: 4
CLB's revised standard version reads **"bare rock."** Seen from the east there is an outstanding bare rock. The name has been applied to a strait that makes the cape an island, and to a section of the City of Gloucester.

ASSABET (River)

Assa - turn back; **be** $\approx$ pe (from nippe) - river; **t** - locative ending. (Pawtucket)

Where the river turns back

In Concord the Assabet joins the Sudbury to form the Concord River, but at high water it reverses the Sudbury and flows upstream into the Sudbury marshes.
Maynard to Concord
1. At the miry place.   JCH
2. It is miry.   RAD-L
See JHT 3, page 16

ASSINIPPI

Assin $\approx$ (h)assun - small stones; **nippi** - brook. (Nipmuck)

Stony brook

(from which the village takes its name)
On Route 3 north of Hanover.
See JHT 1, page 14

ASSONET

Asson ≈ (H)assun - stone; **t** - locative ending. (Nipmuck)

At the stone.

It refers to Dighton Rock which bears a Latin inscription cut by two Dutch explorers cast away on this shore. The rock is submerged at high tide.
I visited it in September 1957 and found it illegible without some means of making the cuts readable.

CAPE POGE

Kup - closed, **pog** ≈ **paug** - pond or place (Wampanoag)

Salt water pond

Enclosed by wind and sea driven sand.
Near Edgartown.
The name has been transferred to the northeast cape of Martha's Vineyard.

CHAPPAQUIDDICK

Chappa ≈ chippi - separate; **qiddick** ≈ aquidne - island. (Wampanoag)

Separate island

The island is separated from Martha's Vineyard by a narrow strait.
East of Martha's Vineyard.

CATAUMET

Cat ≈ **keight** - principle, **aum** - contraction of verb **aumau** - fishing by line, **et** - locative (where there is) Wampanoag

Principle place where there is fishing by line

Village on Buzzards Bay.

CHAUBUNAGUNGAMAUG (Lake)
CHAUBUNAKUNGAMAUG (John Eliot's spelling 1668)

Chaubu ≈ **chippeu** - it divides itself (i.e. a boundary), **gamaug** ≈ **kamok** - a non residential structure to enclose space

A boundary marker
(originally between the Nipmucks and the Narragansetts.)

East of Webster on Connecticut border.
Sometimes called Lake Webster.
JHT caught the reference to fish in the - kungamaug and translated it 'fishing place at the boundary," after which the name was applied to the divided pond. JHT writes further "On some modern maps the name appears as **Chargog gagog manchuga gog**, retaining only a suggestion of its origin and incorporating with it the name of the Indian Village Monulchogok. Aside from this confused etymology the point of interest to us is the fact that the boundary between the Narragansetts and Nipmucks of the seventeenth century is virtually the corner of the Connecticut and Rhode Island state lines with the Massachusetts boundary.

CHEQUESSET

Cheque ≈ chekee - violence, **s** - small; **set** - at or near. (Wampanoag)

Small violence area

Does this indicate some small altercation took place here? West side of Cape Cod near Wellfleet.
1. Great waves because of north wind. JCH;
2.(Queequeshau) He goes leaping. JHT
About 1911, when I was 13, I stopped at the Chequesset Inn. There was a big sand bluff which I climbed, leaped and slid down!

CHICOPEE

Chico ≈ chekee - violent; **pee** - water. (Nipmuck)

Rapids

Chico (chekee) violent, pee = water
North of Springfield.
Violent water (or) or Cedar tree. JCH

COCHICHEWICK (Lake)

Co ≈ ko (implies continuance); **chiche** ≈ chekee - violence; **wick** - place. (Pena)

(Not strictly an Indian place.)

The name was not applied until 1908 and the name, as spelled, does not apply to water . The outlet brook from the lake drops 100 feet to the Merrimack River.
North Andover.
At the swift current. JCH

COCHITUATE (Lake)

Cochi - source; **tu** ≈ (waco)tu - at the head of; **ate** - locative suffix. (Natick)

Source at head of (Sudbury River).

Northwest of the town of Natick.

Place of swift water. JCH

COHASSET

Co ≈ **ko** - continuous; **hass** ≈ **hassun** - stone; **et** - locative suffix. (Natick)

At the stone ledge.

South shore of Massachusetts Bay.

COTUIT

(Previously spelled Coatuit)
Coa ≈ **quona** - long; **tu** - (contraction of tuck) - estuary; **it** ≈ et - locative suffix. (Wampanoag)

At the long estuary.

A village in Barnstable.
1. Long planting place. JCH
2. A praying village. RADL
JHT suggests that it is possibly Kodtuh coag - Cotuit Highlands, shown on a map.

HOUSATONIC

Housa ≈ **wassi** - beyond; **aton** - mountain; **ic** - locative (land.) (Mohigan)

Area beyond the mountain

River and village near Great Barrington.

Over the mountain. RADL
It was discovered by Indians from the west.

HYANNIS

(Wampanoag)
Name of an Indian chief, Iyanough.
Village in Barnstable.

KATAMA (POND)

Kat ≈ keght - great, **ama** ≈ amahs - fish
(Wampanoag)

Great fish(ing) place
Southeast Martha's Vineyard.

MANCHAUG

Manch ≈ **mansk** - fort; **haug** - high place.
  (Nipmuck)

Fort hill

Village and pond in Sutton.
Island of rushes. Where flags grow. .JCH

An earlier form (Monuchchogok) would appear to indicate hill of ash trees. Neither name indicates water. The pond is over a mile from the village.

MANOMET

Man - high; **manom** - height; **et** - locative ending. (Wampanoag)

At the look-out place

Village southeast of Plymouth.
Cedar swamp. JCH

MASHPEE

Mash ≈ **mass** - great or greater; **pee** ≈ **(nip)pe** - water (Wampanoag)

The greater cove

The town is located at the south or greater part of Wakeby Lake.
Town on upper Cape Cod.
1. Great pond. RAD-L
2. Land near great cove. JCH

MASSACHUSETTS

Mass - great or greater; **achu** ≈ **adchu** - mountain or hill; **ett** ≈ **et** - locative suffix.

The great hill.

The reference is to Blue Hill in Milton
The second English colony in the New World!

1. At the great hill.   RADL
2. At the place of large hills. JCH
The name without the final 's' applied to a tribe in Milton. The colonists added the 's' when speaking of them, not the area.

MATTAPAN

(Originally Mattapannock)
Matta ≈ matchey - evil; **pan** ≈ panaeu - it is spread about; ock - land or place. (Natick)

Evil spread about place.

In 1617 a pestilence killed so many Indians in what is now South Boston, that they lay unburied. For many years those who escaped returned to hold memorial services at what became K. Street. In 1630 a ship load of Puritans settled there and called it Dorchester, named for the place they had left in Dorsetshire. Eventually that part of Dorchester was transferred to Boston, and the name, Mattapan, was revived for a village on the
Neponset, without knowledge as to its significance.
1. A sitting down place (for rest after a carry.) DL
2. He sits down (or) End of portage. JCH
JHT thinks it highly probable it referred to the temporary setting down place of the new-comers.

MATTAPOISETT

Matta - bad; **poi** (pohki) - clearing; **set** is a locative suffix. (Wampanoag)

Uncleared area

On the east side of Buzzard's Bay.
1. Resting place or edge of cove. JCH;
2. Resting place after portage. RADL
There is no apparent reason for a portage at this point.

MENEMSHA

Menem ≈ **millum** - between; **sha** ≈ **sjoe** (pronounced 'shaw') - sea. (Norse dialect)

Between sea.

Menemsha Pond is a tidal pond between Vineyard Sound and the Atlantic, with connections to both.
Village and pond on Martha's Vineyard.
"Middle island" , "Lookout cliff", "Sour berries" JCH
The author's family spent several summers in the 1940s with a relative whose home had a view, such as this, of the pond.

MERRIMACK

Merri ≈ millum - between; (m)**ac** - land
(Norse)

Between land. (See alternative below)

The Pennacook tribe was to the north of the
river and the Massachusetts to the south, but the
land between appears to have been in dispute, or
perhaps it was "the in-between river."
Town and river in northeast Massachusetts.

1. Sea land (salt marshes) is my second choice.
CLB
2. Deep place. JCH
3. Deep river.RADL
The town took its name from the river, not for its
location.

MISHAWUM

Mis ≈ mas - large, great, **sha** - parallel sided (as
in the trunk of tree, the side of a long narrow island, the side of a neck or sand bar. ENH pg.
17), **um** - makes an adverb or adjective into a
noun, as "-ness" does in English , e.g. righ-
teousness.

Great Neck

The native name for Charlestown.
Now applied to a part of the city of Woburn .
It was early translated as 'ferry', but in 1886 E.
N. Horsford wrote up the native names of Boston and goes to great length to explain the syllables of Shawmut and Mishawum. Shawmut
draws on the same root **sha -um**   with the locative ending **ut ≈ et** added.

MYSTIC

Mys ≈ mes - great; **tic** ≈ teig - forest. (Norse)

Big woods

This is favored over the alternatives because an early explorer ventured seven miles inland and reported having searched the first range of hills, covered with forests, and he returned, as there was little probability that the settlement would ever extend beyond. (See *History of Melrose* by E. H. Goss, page 17. Published by the City of Melrose, 1902)
Village in Medford and a northern estuary of the Charles River.
1. Great tidal river. JCH
2. Great river. RAD-L
Boston and the surrounding area was relatively open ground.

NABNASSET

Nabo - prefix denoting ten before a digit; **nass** ≈ neese - two; **et** - locative ending. (Nipmuck)

At number 12.

A village and pond in North Chelmsford
Near the dry land , Chestnut tree place; Pond number 12. All three suggested by JCH.
There is nothing in the name to indicate a pond. Perhaps it was a praying village or 12 miles up the Merrimack. It is interesting to note that 'Nabo' is not the word for ten. Ten by itself is 'piuk.'

NAGOG

Nag - (contraction of Naiag) - corner; **og** ≈ ok - land. (Wampanoag or Natick)

Corner of (tribal) **land**.

Village and lake near Acton.
Wampanoag or Natick.
At the sandy place; or Near the path. Both alternatives suggested by JCH.
The name was not applied to the lake by the In-

NAHANT

N' (is demonstrative) - there; **ahan** - out to sea; **t** - locative ending. (Algonkian root)

There it stands out to sea

It is about two miles out from the main shore line.
Peninsular off Lynn.
1. At the point or Twin islands DL;
2. The point or Almost an island. JCH
'Nahanton' was the Sachem of this area. Was the name given for him or his name taken from the area?

NANTASKET

Nant (adverb denoting) - thereat; **ask** - grass (from masket); **et** locative ending. (Natick)

There it is grassy

Village in Cohasset.
At the strait or Place of ebb tide. JCH
The name stands in contrast to rocky Cohasset.

NANTUCKET

(Spelled NIANTICUT by Roger Williams, 1636)
Nai - angle; **an** ≈ an(in) - excessive; **tuck** - tidal run; **et** - locative ending. (Wampanoag)

Tidal run around a sharp angle

Nantucket harbor is around a point, as opposed to Vineyard Haven, which opens directly on the Sound. (The contrast of places is notable in many Indian place names.)
An island to the south of Cape Cod.
Wampanoag or Narragansettt
In the midst of waters, or At the far off place. JCH
RTS (page 114) suggests: Naaya - to come around a point, and thus in view; tuck - water driven by waves or tide; et is a locative ending... thus, Tidal run from unseen source.

NATICK

(Not a place name, but a tribe.)
West of Boston.
1. Place of hills or Place of our search. DL
2. The place I seek (that is, home.) JCH
The town was set up by John Eliot for his praying
  Indians.
JHT did not give any meaning to it in any of his
  three books.

NEPONSET

Ne - and **et** - at that place; **pon** ≈ pan - spread out;
  (Natick)

At the spread out place

As one goes upstream from Dorchester Bay the
Neponset River narrows and then spreads out be-
tween, what are now, Granite and Dorchester Av-
enues.
Near Milton
RAD-L (page 134) suggests the name was prob-
ably Wunneponset.
At a good fall (i.e. easily passed over.)

NOBSCOTT

N' - there is, **obsco** ≈ apske - rock, **t** - locative
suffix (Natick)

There is rock or ledge there

Village south of Sudbury.

NONATAM

(Natick)

I bless it

A hill between Brighton and Newton where Eliot
first converted an Indian to Christianity.

NONQUITT

Non - (contraction of Nunobpe) - dry land; **quit** ≈ keag - point or place (usually referring to fishing.) (Wampanoag or Narragansett)

Dry or high land fishing place

The map indicates a ridge along the shore.

Village on the west shore of Buzzard's Bay near South Dartmouth.
The syllable "non" could possibly be a transliteration of Namohs, the word for fish.

ONSET

(Most likely a much shortened form of PATTAGONSET)
Patta - cove with narrow inlet; (n)**agon** - sandy; **et** - locative ending. (Wampanoag)

Small cove with sandy projection at entrance.

Village and small cove at head of Buzzard's Bay in Wareham.
At the small round place. JCH
My interpretation and therefore description appears true on a National Geographic map. Literally, 'patta' indicates a spreading of the water as one enters, but in this case it would seem to refer to the sand.

POCASSET

Pukqui - a hole; **ass** - small; **et** - locative ending.
  (Wampanoag)

At the small cove or hole

(As compared with Catamet)
Village and bay in Bourne, Cape Cod.
1. Where widens out. DL
2. Where the stream widens. JCH
Pukqui - a hole. See for example Wood's Hole.

POLPIS

(Wampanoag)

(Probably the name of a local chief.)

It may be much shortened, but it does not have a locative ending that denotes either water or an area. Thoreau knew an Indian with the name Joseph Polis.
Village and small bay East Nantucket.
Branching harbor.   JCH

PONKAPOAG

Pongqui - shallow; **pog** ≈ paug - pond (Natick)

Shallow pond

Village and pond in Canton.
1. A spring that babbles up from red soil. DL
2. Clear open pond. JCH

POPPONESSIT

Poppo ≈ poquo - opening or hole; **nessi** ≈ neese - two or double; **t** - locative ending. (Wampanoag)

At the double entrance hole

A map indicates one opening has been closed (by tidal
action.)
Beach and bay in Mashpee.
Place of obstructed inlet, or Place of frost fish. JCH
Words with double 's' usually indicate 'small.'

QUANNAPOWIT

A considerably shortened form of an Indian name of the Nipmuck who sold off a lot of Salem land.

A lake in the town of Wakefield.

At the time of King Philip's War there were five recognized Indian nations in southern New England. The Nipmucks lived in Central Massachusetts and appear to have acknowledge supremacy to the Wampanoags and Massachusetts, from which, perhaps, they divided some time earlier.

SAGAMORE

(This is an Indian word signifying a chief, but not a place name.)
It was applied by the English as a proper noun.
Village and beach in Bourne, Cape Cod.
DL on page 346 lists several sagamores.

SANTUIT

As constructed it is not an Indian place name.
(Wampanoag)

Forested

(as opposed to much open sandy places on the Cape.)
This is a very much altered word, probably from Mashantackuck to Shantuck, meaning 'much wooded place.'
Village near Mashpee.
Cool water place. JCH
The name is possibly from a personal name, Sanksuit,
according to DL on page 347.

SAUGUS

(E)**sogoo** - fish weir; **s** - diminutive (Natick)

At the small fish weir

The town and river in north of Boston.
1. Small outlet, extended. DL
2. The outlet." JCH.
I feel that since every river has an outlet, that alternatives are not helpful in identifying a place, while a fish weir is something recognizable.

SCITUATE

(Mo)**skitu** - grass; **ate** ≈ auk - land (Wampanoag)

That which is green

As seen from the sea the four cliffs were grassy as contrasted with Cohasset.

The town southeast of Boston.
1.'Satuit'- Cold brook. DL
2. Cold brook or possibly Slack water (between tides.)   JCH

SEEKONK

See ≈ Shwee - three; **onk** - upright; The first 'k' is connective. (Wampanoag)

Three upright

Probably three markers of the boundary line.

A town on the Massachusetts - Rhode Island state line.
Outlet or mouth of stream, or possibly Wild goose. JCH

SEGREGANSETT

Saagaro - difficult; **kann** - to do; **et** - locative ending. (Narragansettt/Norse dialect)

Difficult to do

(Probably a difficult place to pass.)
The 'et' is a locative ending, but not a river place.
A village in Dighton.
Place of hard rocks, (or) Where it pours out. JCH

SIASCONSET

Sia ≈ Sidha - (which is Norse for) coast; **skona** - lantern (Wampanoag/ Norse dialect)

Coast lantern or **light house**

Village on the east end of Nantucket Island.

SWAMPSCOTT

(**M')squi** - red; **ompsk** - rock; **ott** ≈ et - locative ending. (Wampanoag)

At the red rock

The red rocks are in Lynn. This name was applied by the town's people when they separated from Lynn.
Town next to Lynn.
(Editor's Note: See "About the Author" CLB arrived at Egg Rock, pictured here between 1 a.m. and 2 a.m.)

TEATICKET

Tea ≈ (keh)te - great; **tick** ≈ tuck - salt river (estuary); **et** - locative ending (Wampanoag)

At the great estuary

Now called Great Pond, but the village today is near one of the lesser inlets.
Village in East Falmouth, but not where the Indians designated.
An alternative name for the place is Tehticut.

WAMESIT

Wame - for all (enough); **sit** - locative suffix.
(Natick dialect: Pawtucket tribe.)

There is enough for all

Village in Tewksbury.
1. Praying village, a place for all. DL
2. There is room for all. JCH

WAQUOIT

Waquo ≈ wehque (a preposition) as far as; **it** (locative suffix) - at (Wampanoag)

This must be a contraction by the English, since the name does not include either a noun or a verb which would include useful information.

Village in East Falmouth.
"At the end" JCH

WAUWINET

(Wampanoag)

The name of a Sachem, Isaac, son of Nicanoose.

Village in E. Nantucket.
See DL page 363

WIANNO

(Wampanoag)

The name of a Sachem, variation of Iyanough of Cummaquid.

Village on the south side of Barnstable.

WORONOCO

(WORONOAK) (Nipmuck)
Local people suggest the alternative spelling and following meaning of the word:

"Place where the salmon jump."

(It may be a fact that salmon jump there, but it is not the etymology of the word.)
Village in Russell.
JHT says that if this is an Indian word it probably has been transferred from some other locality.
An "ak" ending implies "land".

NOTES

ACQUIDNET
AHQUINEY

Aquid - island, **et** - locative suffix (Narragansett)

At the island

The name of Rhode Island in the early years.

This word differs from the more common **'menah'** or **'mon'** which denoted a mound, in that it referred to an island tied into to other land and surrounded by water as distinguished from a monadnock.

ASHAWAY

(N)**ashaue** - in the middle (East Niantic)

In the middle   (Questionable)

It may be as suggested, but the present village is not between any rivers. It may well be that it is not at the point to which the name originally applied; or it may signify an area between R.I. and Conn. or Narragansett and Pequots.
River and village eight miles north east of Westerly
Land between. JCH
There is no indication in this name as to what is meant.

CANONCHET

(A person's name) (Narragansett)

This was the name of a son of Miantunomoh. He was killed by the English in 1675.
Brook, lake and village in Hope Valley.

MATUNUCK

Mat - no(thing); **un**(ca) ≈ onkoue - beyond; **uck** - locative suffix (Narragansett)

End of the trail.

Village on the shore of Block Island Sound.
Observation place. JCH

MISQUAMICUT

Mishsquammauyok (Plural) - red fish, salmon
(Narragansett)

At the salmon place

East of Watch Hill on R.I. Sound

I am not sure that this is the original locus for the
name. Fishing was usually done in rivers.
See JHT 3, page 59 for source of meaning.

NARRAGANSETT

Narra ≈ naiag - point of land; (Naiagans is the diminutive); **et** - locative suffix (Narragansett)

Small point of land

Town on the west side of the bay. Narragansett Pier is a summer colony.
The name originally referred to Point Judith Pond, but which of several points is not certain. It was the tribal seat of the Nahicans.

NAYATT

Nai (verb) - it makes a point; **att** - (locative suffix) - at (Narragansett)

At the point

South of Barrington at the upper end of Narragansett Bay

PASCOAG

Pasco (variant of) peske - divided; **ag** (variant of) auke - land (Nipmuck)

Divided land (possibly) **Boundary**

Old map indicates a lot of brooks.
A river, reservoir and town.
The dividing place. JCH
JHT appears to be in error about the location. The Blackstone River is nowhere near Pascoag of today and the locative ending does not imply a river setting.

PAWTUCKET

Paw - falls (literally 'loud noise'); **tuck** - salt water; **et** - locative suffix (Narragansett)

At the falls into salt water

City and reservoir
At the falls. DL
The Blackstone River in North Providence falls into the upper Narragansett Bay.

PESQUAMSCOT

Pedke - divided (cleft), **amsco** - rock, **t** - locative ending. (Narragansett)

At the cleft rock

South Kingston

NOTES

ASPETUCK

Aspe - high; **tuck** ≈ tauk - land (Paugusett)

The ridge which divides the two branches

Village north of Westport and at the river.

High place.   JCH
This is a variant of Ashpohtag - Eliot, according to JHT 2, page 6.
Here is an example of the problem of transliteration. "**tuck**" as a suffix usually translates as tidal pool, whereas **"tauk"** means land. One must know something of the geography to guess at which sound was originally being written. The first syllable and the map indicate the word did not imply a tidal river, but some formation of land.

CONNECTICUT

Conne ≈ Quinne = long; **ticu** ≈ tegw ; **t** = at.

At the long river

The area bordering that river.
JHT comments the 'c' in the second syllable has no business there.

COS COB

Cassacub- high rock (JHT 2 pg. 12)

High rock

A name transferred to the village and harbor in Greenwich.

HIGGANUM

(Tom)hegan - tomahawk: **tom** - ax; **hegan** - instrument (Mohegan)

Tomahawk

A village west of the Connecticut River, southeast of Middleton
A longer name indicated 'rock for axes.' The full name appears near Moosehead Lake, Maine.

MASHANTUCKET

Masha≈ mass - great; untaug - wood; et - locative ending (Mohegan - Pequot)

At The Place of Much Wood

JHT pg. 25
"Place of Big Trees" JCH pg 99
Originally applied to an area at Killingly. JHT
The tribal name and reservation at Ledyard on which a casino is located.
(This is a posthumous addition from the author's handwtitten notes.)

MASHAPAUG

Masha ≈ mass - great; **paug** - pond (Nipmuck)

Great pond

On the State line south of Sturbridge, MA.

MASSAPEAG

Massa - great or greater; **pe** ≈ (nip)pe) - river; **ag** - ≈ auk - land (Mohegan)

Land by the great river.

Village on the west side of the Thames River.

Place at the large cove. JCH

MAY LUCK

Namelake or namareck ≈ **N ' amau** - there is fish ,
y - (connective), **ake** - locative ending

This is a fishing place

East Windsor

MOHEGAN   (formerly Pequots)

Wolf tribe

(It is not an Indian place name.)
West of Thames, north of Uncasville.
Tribal chief: Uncas; Indian preacher: Occum

MONTOWESE

(Quinnepiac)

Not an Indian place name.

It is derived from the words **Manitou** = "Little god" and "**Sowheag**," a sachem."   JHT 2, page 32
Village between New Haven and North Haven.

MOODUS

(Mache) moodus: **mache** - bad; **moodus** - noise (Wangunk)

Bad noise

Did the name apply to earth movement or to early manufacturing noise? There are reportedly limestone caves in the area which may have contributed, in some way, to the noise.
Village and reservoir, East Haddam.
JHT History of Connecticut, Vol. II pp 91-92

MOOSUP

(Narragansett)

An alternate spelling of Mausup, a Narragansett sachem.

Village and pond, north of Plainfield.

MYSTIC

Mys ≈ mes - great; **tic** ≈ tieg - woods (Norse dialect Mohegan tribe)

Great woods

The old town is probably the locus of the original name.
Town between Groton and Stonington.

Lemoin, a Canadian Missionary, suggests the meaning.

NAUGATUCK

Nauga - single; **tuck** ≈ tungk - tree
(Quinnepiac)

Single tree

1. Tidal river JHT
2. One tree   RAD-L
NOTE: '-tuck' usually refers to an estuary, but
JHT 2 (page 36,) quotes "Nau-ka-tungk" as an
earlier spelling.
Oddly, the modern spelling applies to an estuary
near Stratford.

NIANTIC

Nian ≈ nayan - corner or angle; **tic** ≈ tegw -
river (Narragansett and Mohegan)

Bend in the river

Village and river east of Lyme.
Point of land on estuary. JCH
JCH's meaning fits better than my etymologi-
cal one based on the map, a point on the shore
rather than a bend in the river.

NOANK

N ' - there (at) **oan** ≈ ohan - out to sea; **k** -
locative suffix indicative of land. (West Niantic)

There out to sea (That is, A point of land)

A point on Long Island Sound. Village west side
of the Mystic River.
1. Corner, angle or point. RAD-L
2. It is a point. JCH

ONECO

(Mohegan)
The name of a son of the Sachem, Uncas.
Village near Sterling

PATTAQUONK

Puttu - round, **quonk** ≈ **kakaun** - sweat house

At the round place

JHT 2 pg 65
In the town of Chester there is a hill on which there used to be an Indian sweat-house in the shape of a wigwam or tower.

PAWCATUCK

Pawca ≈**Pequot** - Pequot; **atuck** ≈ tauke - land
JHT 1 pg. 6 (Pequot or eastern Niantic)

Pequot territory

Village and river on R.I. State line

1. Clear tidal run. JHT
2. Clear divided tidal stream.   JCH
The author prefers JHT 2.

PEQUABUCK

Pequab ≈ Pequot; **uck** ≈ auke - territory
  (Wampanoag)

Pequot territory

Village west of Bristol.
The Farmington River originally carried this
  name.

PONSET

(Possibly COCKAPONSET - Barber, see below)
Cocka ≈ **kooche** - source; **pon** (JHT gives no clue); **set** - near; (West Niantic)
(The meaning is obscure)
Southwest of Haddam
1. At the falls.   JCH
2. Barber's Historical Collection pg. 515, thinks the whole name might have been Cockaponset which would translate 'Near source.'
My map indicates two brooks flowing in opposite directions. Is there a swamp?

POQUETANOCK

Pohque - clear(ed); **an** - by labor (shortened); **ock** - land (Mohegan)

Plowed ground

Cleared by labor land.
Village south of Norwich.
Local tradition suggests 'Cracked in dry season' JCH

POQUONOCK

(Several dialects: Mohegan and Paugusset)
(see above)

Cleared land

The meaning is similar to Ponquetanock

Land of defeat. JCH

QUINEBAUG

Quine - long; **baug** ≈ paug - pond (Nipmuck)

Long pond

River and Village southwest of Webster, MA.

The river rises in Massachusetts and flows south to the Thames. The only pond is a slight widening of the river and the village is several miles north of the "pond."

SAUGATUCK (PAUGUSSET)

Sauke - outlet, **tuc** - tidal, **k** - locative suffix

At the tidal outlet (i.e. estuary)

See note on Aspetuck river.
Here is the correct use of the final syllable.

TACONIC

Ta ≈ tagh - wild; **con** - forest; **ic** - locative ending (Mohigan or Natick)

Wild forest

Village south of Salisbury.
JCT 2 pg. 68 says, "Of a dozen probably meanings that might be suggested, I cannot affirm
any."
FHE found it difficult to analyze, but thought it
might have to do with where one could cross a
river. Another suggested meaning is Rough
Country.

UNCOWA

ongkoue - beyond (Paugusset)

Beyond   (the Penquonnuc River)

Fairfield County (but not on my maps.)
JHT 2 pg. 75

WEATOGUE

Weato ≈ weeta - wigwam; **gue** ≈ auke - place;
(Tunxis)
Camp site

I rely on JHT 2 pg. 80. **Wea** = round about;
togue - river.
Round about river

The Farmington branches start in Massachusetts
and flow south. The Farmington River turns
north at Farmington through Weatogue and on to
Tarffville, then east and south to the Connecticut
River at Windsor.   Farming towns in fact! An-
other case of contrast: Connecticut - "long"" vs.
Weatogue - "round about."
Village northwest of Hartford on the Farmington
River
1. Camp site. JHT 2 page 80

WEQUETEQUOCK

Weque - at the end; **tequ** - river ; **ock** - land or
area; (Mohegan)

Area at the river boundary

The Pawtucket river is the boundary between CT
and
R.I. Now an exit on Interstate 95.
Opposite Westerly, R.I.

WILLIMANTIC

Willi ≈ **wewe** - round about; **mantic** - look out (or)
place of observation (Mohegan)

Wide range look-out

There are three rivers converging at this point.
River and village at the junction of routes 32 and
19
1. Good look-out place. JHT
2. Good cedar swamp. JCH

WONGUNK

wonkad - that which is bent JHT 3, pg. 225
(Mohegan)

That which is bent

The bend referred to is in Glastonbury on the
Connecticut river which for the most part is
quite straight.

WUNNECUNSET

wunnaug - bowl, **un** - beyond, **set** -place
JHT 2 pg. 92

Beyond bowl place

Lebanon
JHT was not sure as the name appears to be that
of a hill or some hollow near it.

NOTES

Root	Equivalent ≈ or Alternative	Meaning	Author quoted	Notes
ac	≈ ook	water : suffix often meaning harbor	FHE page 50	
adn	aten	mountain	JL 16	Abnaki
aga	affi	other side or over across	FHE 181	
agua		beneath	FHE page 255	
ak		above	RTS 1 pg 8	Norse
amago	≈ amaug	fish	JHT 3 page 7	
amkeag		sandbar, often locus weir	JHT1 page 40	
anis		branch	FHE	
anna	Possible ≈ (W)inne	smooth	CLB	not found except in personal names
apsk		rock	FHE page 45	
aroos	See walas	shallow	JL 206	
ask	≈ askaskw	green	JL page 45	

Root	Equivalent ≈ or Alternative	Meaning	Author quoted	Notes
bac	≈ bag, ≈ bagat	still water	FHE page 162	
bem	≈ pem	extended or long	FHE page 103	
bungamuin		**boundary**	**FHE 152**	
cara	≈ kara	scrape	RTS 1 page 27	
chebe	≈sebe	divided	FHE page 255	
con	≈ (pa)gon	nut	GMD	Journal of American Linguistics
cook	see -ook			
coos	≈ kowas	pine tree	JHT 3 page 307	
egon		ridge	FHE page 104	(Micmac) W.F. Ganong
esogw		weir	FHE page 15	(Maliseet)
esq				
ey		island?		
ge	ke	denotes continuation or extending		

Root	Equivalent ≈ or Alternative	Meaning	Author quoted	Notes
hegan	≈ agon ≈ egon	open sea	FHE 97	
hook + ?		hook, shell	N. H. Town names	(anna)
jep	≈ dge	rapids	FHE page 151	
k		locative suffix where		
ka		where	JL page 209	Iraquois
kabasse		sturgeon	JL page 39	
kad	≈ kat	eel	FHE page 87	
kaht	≈ keht	principal	FHE page 140	
kamigo		ridge	FHE page 73	
kantti		plenty	JHT 1 page 25	
keag		point or bar where weirs were built for fishing	JHT 1 page 41	
kenne		long	FHE page 142	

Root	Equivalent ≈ or Alternative	Meaning	Author quoted	Notes
looneskw		clay	FHE 164	There is no "l" in contemporary native language. This may be an example of a word that was misunderstood by the early translators.
m'squi		red	JHT 3 page 313	
mada		worn out, poor	FHE page 73	
mad	mag	big	FHE 73	Micmac
magwin		swelling	FHE 72	
maladagw		cedar	FHE 127	
man	≈ menahan	island, look-out	JL page 16	
manan		island	FHE 104	Micmac
manza	maza	white	FHE 164	Micmac ?
mata		at the mout of	FHE 87	
matche		bad	FHE 73	Abenaki
matin		cut off	FHE page 97	
med	met	at the end of	FHE 73	

Root	Equivalent ≈ or Alternative	Meaning	Author quoted	Notes
medames		alewives	FHE page 106	
meddy	≈ medon	alewives	FHE page 106	
menahan		island	JL 16	
molle	≈ mille	deep	FHE 182	
mon	mun	trench-like with sheer walls	FHE 116	
monhi	≈ moni	ample	RTS 1 page 107	(Norse)
moosi		smooth	JHT 3 page 66	Natick
nahmays		fish page147	FHE	Abenaki
namas		fish	JL page 39	Abenaki
nashoue		between or half way	JHT 2 page V	
nic	≈ naghe	island		
nippe		water, usually not flowing	JHT 1 page 14	
nock	≈ tatnock	marsh (grass)	FHE 181	
Noreg		Norse	RTS 1, page 252	
nuppoh		wing	JHT 3 p 97	
(un)nussu		shaped		
obsc	≈ apske	rock	FHE page 2	

Root	Equivalent ≈ or Alternative	Meaning	Author quoted	Notes
ock		locative ending (water)		
ogun	≈ oban	sand bar	FHE page 176	
ohnawa		current (swift)	JL 209	
olamon		vermillion	FHE page 46	
ook -		locus suffix indicating water	FHE page 57	When preceded by 'c' or 'k' sand is indicted.
ook		words ending thus indicate a larger body of water or pool		Abenaki see ticook
os	≈ coos	pine		
pan		spread out	FHE page 50	
panneussu		wrong, unjust	JHT 3 page 110	
pe	≈ pen; ≈ pemi	entended	FHE page 102	

Root	Equivalent ≈ or Alternative	Meaning	Author quoted	Notes
passad		above, upstream	FHE page 47	
quit	≈ keag which forms	a sandy point page 177 a lagoon	FHE	
quoddy	≈ akadi	plenty	FHE page 227	
s				added to a noun indicates diminutive size; before location. As a suffix it indicates 'near.'
sa	≈ chi	big	FHE page 50	
sauk(ee)		outlet	JHT 1 page 32	
sepe	≈ sippe	river	JHT 3 page 148	Consider similarity to Mississippi
scot	≈ apske	rock	FHE page 151	
sco		watching place	FHE page 126	
se	≈ mesi	great	JL page 65	
sebe(se)		brook	JL page 40	
segan		narrows	FHE 117	

Root	Equivalent ≈ or Alternative	Meaning	Author quoted	Notes
sjoe	sea or tide	RHS1 p 276		Norse, pronounced 'shaw'
s				in Penobscot represents "k " as a suffix.
tick	≈ tegw	river	JL page 16	
ticook	tegw	brook		Abenaki (with locative suffix)
timakwa		beaver	JL page 36	
togus	ticus	river		short form for longer name
toocoo	≈ tegw	river	GMD	
tun	≈ tuun	enclosed field	RTS 1 page 319	(Norse)
utn	≈ adne	mountain	JL page 16	
walagaskoo		bark	JL page 32	
walas		shallow	JL 206	Abenaki
walini		curve or cove	FHE 6	

Root	Equivalent ≈ or Alternative	Meaning	Author quoted	Notes
wasset		seething	JHT 3 page 182	
willi	≈ wli	good	JL page 65	
win		good, smooth	JHT 1 page 32	
winos		onion	JL page 43	
wis	**≈ wetchi** sankessuh	**where** one comes out	**Rev. O'Brian**	**The** meaning differs from "sauk" in that it is obscure.
wock	≈ folk		RTS 1 page 282	Norse
wytopi	≈ wyopi	alders	JL 32	

Root	Equivalent ≈ or Alternative	Meaning	Author quoted	Notes
acco		on the other side	JHT 1 page 10	
ack	auk	land, place area	JHT 1 page 6	
ag	auk			
agwe		below or beneath	JHT 3 page 225	
am	um (makes an adverb into a noun)		ENH page 15	
an (eu)		excessive	JHT 3 page 12	
ask		grass	JHT 3 page 64	
aspe	≈ ashpe	high	JHT 2 page 6	
assa		turn back	JHT 3 page 16	
assin	≈ hassun	stone	JHT page 27	
aton	≈ adene	hill or mountain	JHT 2 page 15	
aum	aumau	fishing by line	JHT 3 page 18	See foot note[1]
be	≈ pe; ≈ (nip)pe	river or standing water	JHT 1 page 34	
cat	≈ keht	great(er) by comparison	JHT 3 page 271	
chappa	≈ chippi	separate	JHT 3 page 319	
chekee		violently	JHT 3 page 22	
chochi		source	JHT 3 page 44	
choco				see "chekee"

[1] Before the colonists introduced fish hooks most fishing was done by building weirs and shutting the gates as the tide or current backed out. My Native assistant, while surveying for the Hortonia Power Co. in Vermont, once showed me how he could catch a fish bare-handed in a shallow pool.

Root	Equivalent ≈ or Alternative	Meaning	Author quoted	Notes
co		denotes imperfect present, i.e. "continuing"	JHT 3 p. 87	
Conne	(see Quinni)			
hassun		stone	JHT p.27	
haug	≈ auk	dry ground, area	JHT 2 p. viii	
higan	≈ h'gen	device	JHT 3 p. 97	
housa	≈ wussi	beyond	JHT 2 p. 15	
ic		(locative suffix - see "ak")	JHT 1 p. 42	
k				sometimes used as a connective
kann		to do	RTS 2 p.126	
kodtuh-koag		high place	JHT 3 p.276	
kup	kuppi	shut or closed in	JHT 3 p 43	
man		high place	JHT 2 p. 89	
manch	≈ mansk	fort	JHT 3 p.263	
mashen	≈ mishun	much wooded	JHT 2 p. 25	
mass	≈ miss, ≈ mess	great(er)	JHT 2 p. 26	
masket		it is grassy	JHT 3 p. 64	
mat		no(thing)	JHT 3 p. 51	
matta	≈ matche ≈ mache	bad or evil	JHT 3 p. 50	
menem	≈ millum	between	RTS 1 p.276	
merre	≈ merei	sea	RTS 1 p.277	

Root	Equivalent ≈ or Alternative	Meaning	Author quoted	Notes
millum	≈ mirrum ≈merrim ("l" and "r" interchangeable)		RTS 1 p 276	
mis	≈ mas	large, great	ENH p 14	
moodus		noise	JHT 2 p. 18	
m'squi		red	JHT 3 p.313	
(mo)sskitu		grass	JHT 3 p. 64	
mys	≈ mest	large	RTS 2 p.170	
n'		there-at (demonstrative)	JHT 3 p. 73	
nabo		ten	JHT 3 p. 73	
nagon		sand	JHT 3 p. 74	
nai	≈ narra	corner or angle	JHT 2 p. 35	
nan	≈ nian, nayan	corner or point	JHT 3 p. 74	
nashaue		between, in the middle	JHT 3 p. 77	
neese		two	JHT 3 p. 81	
nippe		water (in compound words)	JHT page 14	
non	≈ nunopi	dry land	JHT 3 p. 97	
obsk	ompsk	rock	JHT 3 p.106	
oc	og, auk	land	JHT 2 p. 6	
om	um	makes an adverb a noun	ENH p. 15	
onk		upright (post)	ENH p. 18	
onkoue		beyond	JHT 3 p.107	

Root	Equivalent ≈ or Alternative	Meaning	Author quoted	Notes
ot	et	exact (location suffix)	JHT 1 p. 24	
pasco	≈ peske	(in compound names) divided	JHT 1 p. 11	
patta	≈ kakaun	round	JHT 2 p. 45	
paug	pog	pond	JHT 1 p. 15	
patta	putte	round	JHT 2 p. 45	
paw		falls (literally) loud noise	JHT 1 p. 9	
pawca	≈ Pequot		JHT 2 p. 46	
pongqui		shallow	JHT 3 p.130	
poppo		hole	JHT 3 p.278	(c.f., Woods, H.)
pukqui		hole		
quinni	≈ conne	long	JHT 1 p. 8	
quit	keag	point (fishing)	JHT 1 p.42	(a spear or spit?)
quonk	≈ kakaun	wigwam or structure		
saagaro		difficult	RTS 2 p. 126	(Norse)
sauki	saugi		JHT 1 p 32	See note 2

2 In composition with 'tuk' implied an estuary. As a noun, often implied a weir place.

Root	Equivalent ≈ or Alternative	Meaning	Author quoted	Notes
sha		parallel sided	ENH p 17	as in tree trunk, sides of long narrow islands, neck or sandbar
shwe	≈see	three	JHT 3 p 149	
sia	sidha	coast	RTS 1 p 298	(Norse)
skona		lantern	RTS 1 p.299	
set		(approximately)	JHT 1 p. 24	location suffix "near"
's'		added to a noun it indicates diminution		
sjoe		sea	RTS 1 p. 276	(Norse)
tee	(keh)te, te	great(er)	JHT 3 p. 31	
tick	teig	wooded	JHT 2 p. 25	
tuck	≈tuk	(usually) tidal river	JHT 1 p. ix	
um			ENH p 15	makes an ad verb or adjective into a noun as "-ness" does in English : "righteous ness"
un(ca)	onkoue	beyond	JHT 3 p. 107	
ut	≈ et		ENH p. 15	locative suffix
wame		for all	JHT 3 p.18	

Root	Equivalent ≈ or Alternative	Meaning	Author quoted	Notes
wequo	waque	as far as	JHT 3 p.188	

Day, Gordon M. *THE NAME CONTOOCOOK,* International Journal of American Linguistics (Vol. XXV. pp 272-3.)

Douglass-Lithgow, R.A., LLD *DICTIONARY OF AMERICAN INDIAN PLACE NAMES IN NEW ENGLAND* (Salem Press, Salem MA, 1909)

Eckstorm, Fannie Hardy *INDIAN PLACE NAMES OF THE PENOBSCOT VALLEY AND MAINE COAST,* (University of Maine Studies in History and Government No. 55., Orono, 1941, Reprinted 1960)

Gookin, Warner F. *CAPAWACK, MARTHA'S VINEYARD,* (Dukes County Historical Society, Reynolds Printing New Bedford, 1947)

Horsford, Eben N. *INDIAN NAMES OF BOSTON* (John Wilson and Son, Cambridge, 1886)

Huden, John C. *INDIAN PLACE NAMES OF NEW ENGLAND* (Museum of the American Indian, Heye Foundation, New York 1962)

Hubbard, Lucius L. *WOODS AND LAKES OF MAINE* (James R. Osgood and Co., 1884)

Laurent, Joseph (Abenaki Chief) *ABENAKISS AND ENGLISH* (Leger Brousseau, Quebec 1884)

O'Brian, Father M.C., notes in Portland Historical Society Library, Portland, Maine

Rasles, Father Sebastian *ABENAKIS DICTIONARY* (Prior 1723 The original is in the Houghton Library, Harvard University.)

Sherwin, Reider *VIKING AND THE RED MAN*, Volume 1 (Funk, New York, 1940)

Sherwin, Reider *VIKING AND THE RED MAN,* Volume 2 (Funk, New York, 1942)

Sweetser, M.F. *KING'S HANDBOOK OF BOSTON HARBOR* (Moses King Corp. Publishers and Engravers, 1888)

Trumbull, James Hammond *COMPOSITION OF INDIAN GEOGRAPHICAL NAMES* (Connecticut Historical Society, Hartford, 1870)

Trumbull, James Hammond *INDIAN PLACE NAMES IN AND ON THE BOR-DERS OF CONNECTICUT*   (Case, Lockwood and Brainerd, Hartford, 1881)

Trumbull, James Hammond *NATICK DICTIONARY* (Bureau of American Eth-nology Bulletin 25, Smithsonian Institute, Wash. DC, 1903)

Weeks, Alvin G. *MASSASOIT OF THE WAMPANOAGS* (Privately printed for the Massasoit Memorial Association, 1920)

ABOUT THE AUTHOR

C. Lawrence Bond came to published authorship late in life. In 1989 he completed *A History of the Houses and Buildings of Topsfield,* on behalf of the Topsfield (Massachusetts) Historical Society. It had been a ten year project undertaken after the death of his wife and partner of forty-nine years, Barbara (Dailey). His first book, like this one, was initially prepared on a 1920 vintage Corona typewriter. At age 94 Mr. Bond began to learn how to use a Macintosh computer and used it to transfer his daily diary to computerized form.

Born in Boston in the 19th Century and a resident of Topsfield, Massachusetts from 1930 until the end of his life, he became a repository of an incredible amount of New England history. (He could tell you, for instance, about the brass mileage markers on the island curbstones on Commonwealth Avenue.) A 1920 A.B. graduate of Harvard College and 1922 S.B. graduate of the Harvard Engineering School, he went to work as a civil engineer and land surveyor.

Early in his career, having completed a summer job on Cape Cod, he needed to return a Swampscott dory to the family home at Swampscott. Rather than hiring a truck he rowed! The first night he guided the dory to a safe landing by listening to the sounds of the waves on the darkened beach near Plymouth. The next day he rowed against the wind for five hours to make only nine miles. He went ashore for a meal and to rest until the wind shifted. In late afternoon he set out again, rowing across the mouth of Boston Harbor with no lights. A freighter passed ominously close without ever seeing the bobbing dory. The expedition ended at 2:00 a.m. the next morning when he arrived home in Swampscott.

Through the years he was no less a tenacious and vigorous citizen of Topsfield, both within his professional work, surveying private properties, laying out roads for developments, and as a volunteer, working with the Town Assessors, as a Commissioner of Public Funds, Park Commissioner and as an active member of the Historical Society.

During the summer he was usually found at the Orr's Island Campground in Maine, helping his sons' family corporation by maintaining the property and sharing his knowledge with others.

At age 95 he researched and added fifty entries to this piece of work. He was still working on his next book, an autobiography entitled *Ten Decades,* when his heart was stilled and he entered peacefully into his final rest.

A.B.B.

C. Lawrence Bond at age 93 with the first edition of this book.